Eclipse: 30 Half-Mandalas For Colouring

Delyth Angharad

ISBN-13:
978-1984975874

ISBN-10:
1984975870

PDF Downloads:

You can download PDFs of both the full- and half-mandalas from the below links.
Note that these are provided only for your personal colouring use; please don't share
the links. If you'd like to direct someone to a link where they can buy the digital
downloads, see the Etsy link below. <3

Full Mandalas: **https://tinyurl.com/eclipsefullmandalas**

Half Mandalas: **https://tinyurl.com/eclipsehalfmandalas**

BUY THE DIGITAL DOWNLOAD PACK ON ETSY:

https://tinyurl.com/etsyeclipse